GEORGE WASHINGTON WASN'T THE FIRST PRESIDENT

EXPOSING MYTHS ABOUT US PRESIDENTS

BY KATE MIKOLEY

Gareth Stevens
PUBLISHING

Please visit our website, www.garethstevens.com. For a free color catalog of all our high-quality books, call toll free 1-800-542-2595 or fax 1-877-542-2596.

Library of Congress Cataloging-in-Publication Data

Names: Mikoley, Kate, author.
Title: George Washington wasn't the first president : exposing myths about US
    presidents / Kate Mikoley.
Description: New York : Gareth Stevens Publishing, 2020. | Series: Exposed!
    More myths about American history | Includes index.
Identifiers: LCCN 2018051087| ISBN 9781538237502 (pbk.) | ISBN 9781538237526
    (library bound) | ISBN 9781538237519 (6 pack)
Subjects: LCSH: Washington, George, 1732-1799–Juvenile literature. |
    Presidents–United States–Biography–Juvenile literature. | United
    States–History–Errors, inventions, etc.–Juvenile literature.
Classification: LCC E312.66 .M54 2020 | DDC 973.4/1092 [B] –dc23
LC record available at https://lccn.loc.gov/2018051087

First Edition

Published in 2020 by
Gareth Stevens Publishing
111 East 14th Street, Suite 349
New York, NY 10003

Designer: Sarah Liddell
Editor: Therese Shea

Photo credits: Cover, p. 1 (background photo) photo courtesy of Library of Congress; cover, p. 1 (George Washington and Abraham Lincoln), 17 (Lincoln) Scewing/Wikimedia Commons; cover, p. 1 (Zachary Taylor) DcoetzeeBot/Wikimedia Commons; cover, background texture used throughout IS MODE/Shutterstock.com; ripped newspaper used throughout STILLFX/Shutterstock.com; photo corners used throughout Carolyn Franks/Shutterstock.com; p. 5 critterbiz/Shutterstock.com; p. 7 US National Archives bot/Wikimedia Commons; p. 9 (Mount Vernon) PhotosbyAndy/Shutterstock.com; p. 9 (silver dollar) Valeri Potapova/Shutterstock.com; p. 11 Luis Molinero/Shutterstock.com; p. 13 Walk Like an Egyptian/Wikimedia Commons; p. 15 Library of Congress/Handout/Archive Photos/Getty Images; p. 17 (John F. Kennedy) WikiPedant/Wikimedia Commons; p. 19 (John Wilkes Booth), 23 (William Howard Taft) Howcheng/Wikimedia Commons; p. 19 (Lee Harvey Oswald) Bradipus/Wikimedia Commons; p. 21 (Theodore Roosevelt) Tom/Wikimedia Commons; p. 21 (teddy bear) NUM LPPHOTO/Shutterstock.com; p. 25 (William Henry Harrison) Mike-Kerkhoven/Wikimedia Commons; p. 25 (Tecumseh) Nikater/Wikimedia Commons; p. 27 Cléééston/Wikimedia Commons; p. 29 Tm/Wikimedia Commons.

Printed in the United States of America

CPSIA compliance information: Batch #CS19GS: For further information contact Gareth Stevens, New York, New York at 1-800-542-2595.

CONTENTS

Words in the glossary appear in **bold** type the first time they are used in the text.

FINDING THE TRUTH

Sometimes stories are told so widely that everyone believes them—even if there's no **proof**! When many people believe an idea that's not true, that idea is called a myth.

You may already know a lot about the presidents of the United States, such as the fact that Abraham Lincoln was the tallest president. But are some of the things you think you know about them just myths? Let's set the record straight about the US presidents!

Mount Rushmore, in South Dakota, shows four US presidents. Do you recognize (from left to right) George Washington, Thomas Jefferson, Theodore Roosevelt, and Abraham Lincoln?

5

WHAT'S UP WITH WASHINGTON?

THE FACTS:

George Washington became president in 1789, but the United States became independent in 1776. So what happened during the time before Washington took office?

The Articles of Confederation served as the first **constitution** for the United States until 1789, when the US Constitution was adopted. Under the Articles, a man named John Hanson became the first president. He served for just 1 year. Washington became the first president under the US Constitution.

REALLY THE PRESIDENT?

Hanson's job was very different from the president's job under the US Constitution. That's why most people still consider Washington the first American president.

THE FACTS:

This tale is sometimes told to show how strong Washington was as a young man. However, this was one feat he never accomplished.

Near Washington's home of Mount Vernon in Virginia, the Potomac River is about 1 mile (1.6 km) wide. That's much too far for anyone to throw an object across. Besides, there were no silver dollars until 1794. That was just 5 years before George Washington's death.

It's possible that Washington threw a piece of slate across the much narrower Rappahannock River. While still not **confirmed**, this story, first told by his grandson, is more likely.

There are narrower areas of the Potomac River, but even the strongest thrower couldn't toss an object across the mile-wide part near Mount Vernon!

THE MYTH:

GEORGE WASHINGTON CHOSE TO BUILD WASHINGTON, DC, ON A SWAMP.

THE FACTS:

It's true Washington chose the location for the nation's capital. However, the idea that it was a swamp is false.

A swamp is a wet area of land that's often covered with water. Washington was skilled at studying land so it would have been strange for him to pick such a poor place. The site was chosen for its location near the Potomac River and several important port cities.

As land was cleared to make room for buildings in Washington, DC, some areas flooded, adding to the myth that the location was a swamp.

While there are some marshy, or wet, areas of land near Washington, DC's rivers, the place was never a swamp.

A TOXIC TALE

ZACHARY TAYLOR WAS POISONED TO DEATH.

THE FACTS:

Zachary Taylor was president for only 16 months. His term was cut short when he died in 1850 after suffering a few days of stomach pain.

Because of his sickness, some people thought Taylor had been poisoned. This would have made him the first president to be **assassinated.** The claim caught so much attention that in 1991 Taylor's body was removed from its grave and studied. Scientists found that he wasn't poisoned.

In truth, Zachary Taylor's death was likely due to a bacterial illness common during the 1800s.

REASON BEHIND THE RUMOR

Taylor's final sickness was similar to what someone would go through if they had been poisoned with **arsenic**. However, these **symptoms** happen with other illnesses, too.

13

THE ENVELOPE ADDRESS

ABRAHAM LINCOLN WROTE THE GETTYSBURG ADDRESS ON AN ENVELOPE WHILE ON A TRAIN ON HIS WAY TO GETTYSBURG, PENNSYLVANIA.

THE FACTS:

There are five known copies of the Gettysburg Address written by Lincoln. None are on an envelope. Plus, they're all written in his normal, neat handwriting. Trains were quite bumpy in Lincoln's time. If he'd written the speech on a train, at least one of these copies would be pretty messy.

A 1906 short story called "The Perfect Tribute" by Mary Raymond Shipman Andrews included this myth. It may be where the myth came from.

Lincoln gave the Gettysburg Address on November 19, 1863, at the location of one of the bloodiest battles of the American Civil War (1861–1865). The speech was given in honor of the national cemetery established there.

Lincoln's Gettysburg Address lasted only 2 minutes, but it's still one of the most famous speeches in American history. Lincoln promised the nation would have a "new birth of freedom."

LINCOLN AND KENNEDY

ABRAHAM LINCOLN HAD A SECRETARY NAMED KENNEDY, AND JOHN F. KENNEDY HAD A SECRETARY NAMED LINCOLN.

THE FACTS:

These two presidents were both killed during their time in office. Over the years, people have claimed they had quite a lot in common. The problem is that many of the claims simply aren't true!

Kennedy did have a secretary named Evelyn Lincoln. But no proof has ever been found to show that Lincoln had a secretary by the name of Kennedy. His secretaries while president were John Nicolay and John Hay.

JOHN F. KENNEDY

ABRAHAM LINCOLN

Some people want to believe that Lincoln and Kennedy had many odd things in common. But many connections just aren't true!

17

THE MYTH:

THE MEN WHO KILLED LINCOLN AND KENNEDY WERE BORN 100 YEARS APART.

THE FACTS:

People often talk about 100-year differences in the lives of Lincoln and Kennedy. Lincoln was elected to Congress in 1846 and Kennedy in 1946. Lincoln was elected president in 1860 and Kennedy in 1960.

But the men who shot the presidents were *not* born 100 years apart. The man who killed Lincoln, John Wilkes Booth, was born in 1838, and the man who killed Kennedy, Lee Harvey Oswald, was born in 1939.

JOHN WILKES BOOTH

WEIRD OR NOT?

You can find similarities between anyone if you look hard enough. People tend to like the number 100, but is it really that weird if things happen 100 years apart?

LEE HARVEY OSWALD

DALLAS POLICE 54018 11 23 63

Some people think it's interesting that the names Lincoln and Kennedy both have seven letters. This fact is true, but it's not very special. Many names have seven letters!

SAVE THE BEAR!

THE FACTS:

Roosevelt did refuse to shoot a bear. However, he didn't save its life.

In 1902, Roosevelt was on a hunting trip. Others had seen bears on the trip, but not Roosevelt. Finally, one was caught and tied to a tree so he could shoot it. But Roosevelt wouldn't, thinking the act would be **unsportsmanlike.** The bear was hurt, so Roosevelt asked for it to be killed to end its pain.

Toymakers made stuffed bears and called them "Teddy's bears" because of the story of Roosevelt refusing to shoot the bear. We call them teddy bears today!

STUCK IN THE TUB?

THE MYTH: WILLIAM HOWARD TAFT, WHO BECAME PRESIDENT IN 1909, ONCE GOT STUCK IN THE WHITE HOUSE BATHTUB.

THE FACTS:

While it's true Taft was a large man, there's no proof this event ever happened. In fact, the myth didn't exist until about 20 years after his term ended.

Taft did, however, bathe in a supersized tub. A specially made bathtub was added to the White House for Taft. At 7 feet (2.1 m) long and 41 inches (1 m) wide, this was much larger than an average tub!

BATHING AT SEA

There are reports of extra-large tubs being added to some boats Taft sailed on, too.

The Taft myth was shared in several books, but historians agree there are no facts to back it up.

A PRESIDENTIAL CURSE?

THE MYTH: BETWEEN 1840 AND 1960, THE PRESIDENTS ELECTED IN A YEAR ENDING IN A ZERO DIED IN OFFICE—BECAUSE OF A CURSE!

THE FACTS:

A myth explains that Native American leader Tecumseh put a deadly curse on future president William Henry Harrison around 1811. Tecumseh was angry because Harrison's soldiers had **defeated** his Shawnee warriors. Harrison, elected in 1840, died in office because of the curse, according to the myth.

Every 20 years after that, the elected US president died in office. The myth doesn't explain why this happened—or why the curse stopped after the 1960 election!

BREAKING THE CURSE?

Ronald Reagan was elected in 1980. Some say he broke the curse when he lived after being shot in 1981.

TECUMSEH

WILLIAM HENRY HARRISON

People like to try to find a reason behind things that seem connected. That's how some myths get started! There's no such thing as the "Tecumseh curse," though.

BECOMING THE PRESIDENT

THE MYTH:

ALL PRESIDENTS MUST BE ELECTED.

THE FACTS:

If the president dies or leaves office, the vice president takes their place. There was one US president who was never elected to either the office of president or vice president, though. That was Gerald Ford!

In 1973, Vice President Spiro T. Agnew left office. President Richard Nixon chose Ford, a leader in Congress, to become the new vice president. The next year, Nixon left office before he could be **impeached.** Ford became president on August 9, 1974.

GERALD FORD

STEPPING INTO THE PRESIDENCY

JOHN TYLER	TOOK OFFICE AFTER DEATH OF WILLIAM HENRY HARRISON IN 1841
MILLARD FILLMORE	TOOK OFFICE AFTER DEATH OF ZACHARY TAYLOR IN 1850
ANDREW JOHNSON	TOOK OFFICE AFTER DEATH OF ABRAHAM LINCOLN IN 1865
CHESTER A. ARTHUR	TOOK OFFICE AFTER DEATH OF JAMES GARFIELD IN 1881
THEODORE ROOSEVELT	TOOK OFFICE AFTER DEATH OF WILLIAM MCKINLEY IN 1901
CALVIN COOLIDGE	TOOK OFFICE AFTER DEATH OF WARREN G. HARDING IN 1923
HARRY TRUMAN	TOOK OFFICE AFTER DEATH OF FRANKLIN D. ROOSEVELT IN 1945
LYNDON B. JOHNSON	TOOK OFFICE AFTER DEATH OF JOHN F. KENNEDY IN 1963
GERALD FORD	TOOK OFFICE AFTER RICHARD NIXON STEPPED DOWN IN 1974

SPOTTING MYTHS

It can be hard to know where myths come from. Some, like George Washington being the first president, may have some truth, but the stories are missing important **details**. Others, like the story of Zachary Taylor being poisoned, may have seemed possible but lack proof.

As time goes on, more myths about American presidents will be passed on. It's important to look for proof and ask questions about odd claims. Don't believe everything you hear!

Over time, true stories can change into myths little by little. Perhaps that's why there are so many myths about early presidents, such as Thomas Jefferson.

ICE CREAM INVENTOR?

Some people think Thomas Jefferson invented ice cream. However, he was just the first president to serve it at dinners!

29

GLOSSARY

arsenic: a poison often used to kill insects or plants

assassinate: to kill someone, especially a public figure

confirm: to find to be true

constitution: the basic laws by which a country or state is governed

defeat: to overcome in battle

detail: a small part of something

envelope: a cover in which letters or other mail are stored

impeach: to charge with misconduct in office

proof: something that shows that something else is true or correct

secretary: a person who works for someone in an office and handles records, letters, and other matters

symptom: a sign that shows someone is sick

unsportsmanlike: not fair or respectful when taking part in a sport or game

FOR MORE INFORMATION

BOOKS

DuMont, Brianna. *U.S. Presidents.* Washington, DC: National Geographic, 2017.

Peacock, L. A. *The Truth (& Myths) About the Presidents.* New York, NY: Scholastic, 2014.

WEBSITES

Presidential Fun Facts
kids.nationalgeographic.com/explore/history/presidential-fun-facts
Find out more interesting facts about US presidents on this site.

United States Presidents
www.ducksters.com/biography/uspresidents
Read the biographies of every US president here.

INDEX